Weight Gain M

Cookbook

CW00494070

Easy And Friendly Weight Gain Meals To Cook, Prep, Grab And Go, With 11 Reliable Step By Step Bulking Meal Prepping Guides.

Bruno Harrison

Table Of Content

INTRODUCTION

A lthough our culture places great importance on thinness, the prevalence of being underweight is a major public health problem. There are several reasons people can be underweight, including genetics and fast metabolism, as well as  underlying medical conditions such as thyroid problems or cancer. Women are at increased risk of being underweight, as are adults over 60

Being underweight poses several health risks, including hair loss, dry skin, fertility issues, and poor dental health. In severe cases, underweight people may have a weakened immune system or develop osteoporosis. Being underweight is linked to a higher risk of death.

The good news is that there are strategies to incorporate nutritious meals into your regular diet that will assist you in gaining weight. Adding more meals and snacks and increasing portion sizes are all ways to get more calories daily. Consuming healthy fats, whole grains, fruits and vegetables, and plenty of water will help you achieve the right weight for you.

Underweight is defined as having a body mass index (BMI) of less than 18.5; a BMI of 18.5 to 24.9 is considered normal.

Body Mass Index (BMI) is an outdated and biased measurement that fails to take into account several factors such as body composition, ethnicity, race, gender, and age.

Although an inaccurate measurement, BMI is widely used in the medical community today as it provides an inexpensive and quick way to analyze potential health issues and their outcomes. Note that being underweight (or overweight) is not always measured by BMI alone, and there are other factors to consider.

Some people are naturally less fat than others and may be perceived as underweight due to their low BMI, but are otherwise perfectly healthy. The same holds true for people whose BMI indicates they may be overweight or obese. It is therefore best to talk to your doctor, who can make an accurate diagnosis.

If you are underweight and it has been determined that your health would benefit from weight gain, your doctor will likely recommend that you eat more nutrient-dense, high-calorie foods to help you gain weight.

To gain weight healthily, you need to consume more calories than your body burns, preferably from nutritious foods. Not all calories are equal and some foods are more nutritious than others.

With that said, I am presenting a personal experience with meal preparation for weight gain in this cookbook. I provided many delicious, incredibly nourishing, and healthy meal suggestions that you can make in advance and store on a weekly or monthly basis.

In addition to these recipes, you need to know the fundamentals of weight gain meal plans, how to prepare meals, and what foods to eat, and what to stay away from, particularly if you are just beginning your weight gain journey. So, I've got all you need to know about the meal-planning strategy for weight gain, along with a tasty selection of recipes.

Section 1: Why You Should Stock Up On Nutritious Foods

It is important to eat nutritious foods, regardless of your weight. The United States Department of Agriculture (USDA) recommends including a variety of nutritious foods in your diet, such as protein, fruits, vegetables, grains, and dairy products for optimal nutrition.

The Food and Drug Administration (FDA) uses a 2,000-calorie diet as an example of nutritional information. Eating 2,000 calories is not necessarily a good recommendation. The number of calories your body needs can vary depending on factors such as age, gender, and activity level.

When you're underweight, you typically want to eat an extra 500 calories a day. This may include eating extra meals or increasing the meals you normally eat. You can also increase calories and fat by adding healthy monounsaturated and polyunsaturated fats like avocados, nuts, seeds, and vegetable oils.

Unless you're particularly hungry, snacking on small, high-calorie snacks throughout the day will likely benefit you. If you're running out of time to prepare extra snacks, you can simply increase the portion sizes of the meals you've already eaten.

While grabbing a bag of savory fries or ice cream might seem like an easy fix, these foods are high in calories but have no nutritional value. Foods rich in sugar and salt might make you feel lethargic and bloated. In addition, regular and excessive consumption of these foods can increase the risk of cardiovascular disease and type 2 diabetes.

Although processed foods are often associated with weight gain and obesity, they can also lead to chronic health problems such as inflammatory bowel disease (IBD), autoimmune diseases, cancer of the colon, and mood disorders, including anxiety and depression.

Instead, start a healthy weight gain regimen using the following tips for eating healthier, more nutritious foods.

Foods That Help You Gain Weight

Some nutritious foods that can help you gain weight are:

- whole milk
- Starchy vegetables
- Avocado
- Creamy soups
- Red meat
- juice

- Cheese
- Nuts and nut butter
- Salmon
- Protein smoothies

What To Eat

1. Eat An Extra Slice Of Whole Wheat Toast With Peanut Butter For Breakfast

Start your day with a hearty breakfast and eat an extra slice or two of whole wheat toast with peanut butter, which is high in calories as well as fat and protein. About 200

 calories are in two tablespoons of peanut butter. Choose natural peanut butter brands over alternatives with added sugar.

Almond butter and other types of nut and seed butter are also healthy choices for weight gain because they are high in protein and high in healthy fats.

Whole grain products are an important source of fiber. Choose whole-grain bread with at least 100 calories per slice. When bread contains nuts and seeds, it generally contains more calories and healthy fats per serving.

2. Drink Whole Milk, 100% Fruit Juice Or Vegetable Juice

Wash down your nut butter toast with a glass of whole milk to add protein, calcium, and vitamin D. If you don't like or

dislike cow's milk, choose a milk alternative made with nuts. It contains fewer calories but still needs to be fortified with calcium and vitamin D, which are important nutrients when you gain weight.

During the day, choose 100% fruit and vegetable juices that do not contain additives such as sugar. Read nutrition labels carefully to make sure you're using real ingredients that you can easily pronounce - the fewer the better.

Sugary sodas can be tempting — and while they're high in calories, they have nothing to offer nutritionally. They're loaded with added sugars, which are linked to an increased risk of chronic disease

For beverages, choose whole milk or fruit and vegetable juices to boost your daily dose of vitamins and minerals.

3. Top Your Avocado Toast With An Egg

Avocado is widely known as a superfood because it is packed with healthy fats and fiber and is an excellent source of

protein. They are an excellent choice for a weight-gain diet. Take your avocado toast to the next level with a fried or poached egg for a double dose of protein and extra calories.

4. Cut An Apple Into Slices And Serve With Nut Butter.

Many people eat too few fruits and vegetables, and although they are lower in calories, you don't want to miss them, as they are also an important part of a balanced diet. Increase your

caloric intake during meals by spreading almond, peanut, or cashew butter on the apple slices. You get lots of nutrients in addition to your calories to help you gain weight.

5. Add Chopped Nuts, Oatmeal, Fruit, And Honey To Yogurt

Enrich your Greek yogurt with a generous helping of walnuts, almonds, or pecans, as well as rolled oats or granola and your favorite dried fruit. Add a spoonful of honey and you have a delicious and healthy snack or dessert.

Yogurt contains beneficial bacteria that help keep your gut healthy, and nuts contain healthy fats and provide the calories you need to gain weight.

6. Pack A Bag Of Trail Mix For A Convenient Snack

Trail mix is a mixture of nuts, seeds, grains, and dried fruits. You can buy trail mix at supermarkets or make your own.

You can even get a few extra calories by adding chocolate chips. Store your trail mix in a plastic bag or container and take it with you on the go so you have something to snack on during your weight gain diet.

7. Increase Protein (And Calorie) Intake With Protein Bars

Protein bars are similar to the ingredients in trail mix. You can make your own protein bars or buy any number of bars at any  grocery store or bakery. Check the nutrition information label to see how many calories you're consuming per serving and if it meets your nutritional needs for weight gain. Also, beware of hidden added sugars.

8. Use Sour Cream as a Go-To Topping

Calcium and extra calories are both included in sour cream, which is necessary for a healthy weight increase. Cheese, gravy, full-fat  Greek yogurt, or grass-fed butter can be used to up the calorie count.

9. Consume More Starchy Veggies Such As Potatoes.

Potatoes have a terrible reputation for being high in carbohydrates, yet your body uses carbohydrates for energy,

and potatoes are high in vitamins, minerals, and fiber. Increase the calories by adding sour cream or yogurt, and earn extra points by cooking with good fats such as olive oil.

Potatoes are on the starchy side, so they also contain more calories than green vegetables. Even if you don't want to skip the Brussels sprouts, broccoli, and kale, feel free to stock up on potatoes, sweet potatoes, pumpkin, winter squash, and even corn.

10. Choose Creamy Soups Over Thin Soups

Baked soups contain more calories than clear broth soups. A big bowl of creamy soup and warm crusty bread can be a great

energy-packed meal when dieting. Boost the nutritional value of your creamy soups by adding vegetables. To do this, choose the cream of broccoli, cream of mushroom, soup, or similar cream soups.

11. Add Cheese Sauces to Greens and Veggies:

Green and colorful vegetables like broccoli are packed with vitamins, minerals, and fiber. But they are also low in

calories. Boost your energy intake by adding cheese or cheese sauce to your favorite green vegetables. If you don't like cheese sauce, consider

roasting your vegetables in olive oil, then tossing them with seeds for extra crunch, fiber, protein, and fat.

12. Eat Red Meat (And Choose Lean Meat For A Healthy Heart)

Although fatty cuts of meat contain more calories, they are also linked to an increased risk of heart disease when consumed in

excess. If you decide to include fatty cuts of red meat in your diet weight, be sure to consider the extent to which.

Lean steaks, lean ground beef, or bison are good options that still contain plenty of nutrients for optimal body function. If you don't eat red meat, you can get your protein from chicken, pork, fish, and even plant-based sources like meat alternatives and legumes.

Whether you choose lean animal protein or plant sources, there are plenty of options to ensure you get enough protein while maintaining your weight.

What to Avoid

When trying to gain weight, a person should be careful to avoid:

Insufficient Cardiovascular Training

Some people stop doing cardiovascular exercise when they're trying to gain weight, but it's important to maintain a healthy heart, lungs, and brain. Running, swimming, and biking are great ways to get cardiovascular exercise.

During your weight gain journey, you can try limiting cardiovascular exercise to around 20 minutes three times a week rather than avoiding it altogether.

A Diet Low In Vegetables

Many types of vegetables fill you up but are low in calories. However, it is crucial not to exclude them from the diet because of weight gain. Vegetables are an important source of vitamins and minerals, and undernutrition can lead to malnutrition.

Give Up Too Soon

Gaining weight safely can take patience and determination. It is not always possible to see instant results. Everyone is different and some may take longer than others.

How To Meal Prep

Despite what people might think, there are many ways to prepare meals, not all of which require spending an entire Sunday afternoon preparing the dishes for the coming week. You can choose the methods that suit you best. Below, we take a look at the basics of meal prepping and break down the process into a few simple steps.

Different Ways To Prepare Food

You may think that cooking for the coming week will take up a large part of your weekend. But because there are different ways to prepare food, you don't have to spend all Sunday afternoon in the kitchen. Everyone will find a suitable style of restoration.

The most popular ways to prepare food are:

Make-ahead meals: Complete pre-prepared meals that can be refrigerated and reheated during meals. This is especially convenient for dinnertime meals.

Batch cooking: Prepare large batches of a specific recipe, then divide them into individual portions to freeze and eat for the next few weeks. These are popular options for a hot lunch or dinner.

Single Portion Meals: Prepare fresh meals and divide them into individual grab-and-go portions to be refrigerated and eaten for days to come. This is especially useful for quick lunches.

Ready-to-cook ingredients: Prepare the ingredients needed for specific meals in advance to reduce cooking time in the kitchen. Which method is best for you depends on your goals and your daily routine.

For example, a ready-to-eat breakfast is best if you want to streamline your morning routine. On the other hand, storing meals in batches in the freezer is especially convenient for those who are short on time in the evening.

The different cooking methods can also be mixed and matched to your own situation. Start by choosing the most appealing method, then slowly experiment with others to see what works best for you.

Picking the right number and variety of meals

It can sometimes be difficult to determine how many meals to prepare and what to include in each meal.

The best way to plan ahead is to first decide which meals you want to focus on and which meal method fits your lifestyle. Then check your calendar to see how many breakfasts, lunches, and dinners you need in the coming week. Also, don't forget to consider when you're likely to eat out, for example, on a date, brunch with friends, or dinner with clients.

When deciding which meals to prepare, it's best to start with a limited number of recipes that you already know. This will facilitate the transition to meal planning. However, it is also important not to choose one recipe for the whole week. This lack of variety can lead to boredom and not providing your body with the nutrients it needs.

Instead, try to choose foods that contain a variety of vegetables and protein foods, as well as a variety of complex carbohydrates, such as brown rice, quinoa, or sweet potatoes. Incorporating a vegetarian or vegan meal into the mix is another way to add variety.

Overview

The correct number of meals depends on your daily routine and your needs. Your body needs a variety of nutrients, including vitamins, minerals, and other health-promoting substances.

Pro Tips For Reducing Cooking Time

Very few people look forward to spending hours in the kitchen cooking. It is natural because the main reason for cooking it is a shorter cooking time.

The following methods will help you optimize preparation and cooking times.

Keep a fixed schedule

Meal prep works best if you stick to a regular schedule. Knowing exactly when to shop and when to prepare meals can help you create a good routine. For example, you can set aside Sunday mornings for grocery shopping and meal prepping. Or you can prepare lunch on Monday evening for the rest of the week.

The schedule is up to you and should fit into your weekly schedule. Remember that choosing specific times and sticking to them will simplify the decision-making process and free up mental space for other things.

Choose The Right Combination Of Recipes

Choosing the right combination of recipes can help you work more efficiently in the kitchen. To save time, choose recipes that require different cooking methods. If you have too many recipes that require the same equipment, e.g. the oven, the number of dishes you can cook at the same time is limited.

This is especially important when choosing to make ahead meals or batch cooking. A good rule of thumb is to stick to one baked meal and up to two burners at a time - say, stuffed baked potatoes, porridge, and soup. Then easily add meals that don't need to be cooked, like sandwiches or salads.

Organize Your Preparation And Cooking Times

A well-thought-out workflow saves a lot of time in the kitchen. To best organize your preparation and cooking times, start with the recipe that requires the longest cooking time. It is often the soup or the oven meals. Concentrate on the rest after the food is ready.

Leave cold meals for last as they can easily be prepared while preparing other meals. To save time, check the ingredients of all recipes before you start. This way, if two recipes call for diced onions or julienned peppers, you can chop the entire amount in one go.

Using automated appliances like a rice cooker or slow cooker can further streamline your workflow.

Write A Shopping List

Shopping can be a huge waste of time. For half the time you spend in the supermarket, keep a detailed shopping list organized by the supermarket department. This saves you from returning to a previously visited section and speeds up your purchase.

Limiting shopping to once a week and using a delivery service are two other ways to spend less time shopping.

Overview

To reduce the time, you spend in the kitchen, stick to a regular schedule and use a shopping list. Choosing the right meal combination and organizing your kitchen is also important.

Choose The Right Storage Container

Your food storage containers can be the difference between a good meal and a mediocre one.

Here are some recommendations for containers:

Airtight Containers for Prepared Ingredients: Washable and reusable silicone bags and stainless-steel containers are ideal for keeping ingredients and food fresh.

BPA-free microwaveable containers: they are both convenient and better for your health. Pyrex jars or collapsible silicone containers are good options.

Freeze Resistant Containers: Reduce freezer burn and food loss. Wide-mouth mason jars are ideal, as long as you leave at least an inch of space for the food to expand when it freezes.

Spill-Proof Containers with Compartments: These are perfect for lunches or meals where ingredients need to be mixed at the last minute. A good example is bento boxes. Stackable or adjustable containers help maximize space in your fridge, freezer, or work bag.

Overview

Containers are practical and space-saving. They can also help your meals taste better and contain more nutrients.

Cook, Store, And Reheat Food Safely

Food safety is an important but overlooked part of cooking. Cooking, storing, and reheating food at the right temperature can prevent foodborne illnesses, which affect an estimated 9.4 million Americans each year.

Here are some recognized federal guidelines for food safety:

Consider appropriate temperatures: keep your refrigerator at 5°C (40°F) or lower and your freezer at -18°C (0°F) or lower.

Chill foods quickly: Always store fresh foods and meals in the refrigerator within two hours of purchasing or preparing them. For rapid cooling, distribute cooked foods in shallow containers and immediately put them in the refrigerator.

Keep storage times in mind: cook fresh meat, poultry, and fish within two days of purchase and red meat within 3 to 5 days. In the meantime, keep them on the bottom shelf of your fridge.

Cook to the right temperature: Meat should be cooked until it reaches an internal temperature of at least 75°C, as this kills most bacteria.

Thaw Foods Safely: Thaw frozen foods or meals in your fridge instead of on your counter. For faster decomposition, immerse food in cold tap water and change the water every 30 minutes.

Reheat food only once: The more often you refrigerate and reheat food, the greater the risk of food poisoning. Thawed food should only be reheated once.

Heat food to the right temperature: All meals should be heated to 75°C before consumption. Frozen meals should be reheated and consumed within 24 hours of thawing.

Use labels: Don't forget to label and date your containers so you can consume the food within the food safety timelines.

Eat on time: Chilled meals should be eaten within 3-4 days and frozen meals within 3-6 months.

Overview

Cooking, storing, and reheating food at the correct temperature can reduce the risk of food poisoning. The guidelines above give you an overview of the most important food safety measures to consider.

Steps For Successful Food Preparation

Preparing food for a week may seem difficult, especially for a beginner. But it doesn't have to be difficult.

Below is a simple step-by-step guide to streamlining your meal prep process.

Choose your diet method: This can be a combination of methods and should be based on your lifestyle and dietary goals.

Stick to a schedule: Pick one day a week to plan your meals, shop, and cook.

Choose the right number of meals: Think about your schedule and the restaurant meals you have planned for the week.

Choose the right recipe: Pay attention to variations and cooking methods. When you start, stick to the recipes you already know.

Save time when grocery shopping: create a shopping list organized by supermarket shelves or shop online.

Spend less time in the kitchen: use cooking time to decide which dishes to prepare first.

Store your meals: Use safe refrigeration methods and appropriate containers. Put the foods you plan to eat within 3-4 days in the fridge, label them and freeze the rest.

Overview

Cooking doesn't have to be complicated. Simple steps can help reduce cooking time and give you more time for the activities that matter most.

Conclusion

The kitchen is good for people who want to spend less time in the kitchen. It can also encourage nutritious and healthy meals and discourage less nutritious fast-food options.

Depending on your goals, schedule, and food preferences, meal prep can mean freezing large portions, storing entire meals in the fridge, or combining prepared ingredients as needed. Find a method that works for you and pick one day a week to plan, shop, and cook.

Section 2: Meal Plans and Recipes

Meal Prep Plan #1:

Chicken Chipotle Burrito Bowls

If you love a good burrito but want to cut your carbs, we have good news for you: it's possible to enjoy all the bold flavors and

textures you're looking for in your favorite burritos without the actual packaging.

These Chicken Chipotle Burrito Bowls are naturally gluten-free and contain far fewer carbs than a traditional flour burrito. But they're still packed with hearty, satisfying ingredients like grilled chipotle chicken, black beans, corn, rice, and all the toppings you know and love.

Burrito bowls are a fun way to build your own dinner bowl so everyone gets exactly what they want. Do you have a child who doesn't like cream? No problem. Does your partner like a good dose of heat? Add spicy salsa to the menu!

The wow factor in this recipe is the chipotle mixture on the grilled chicken. It adds a rich, savory flavor to the chicken and helps keep the chicken moist while cooking. Along with this key flavorful ingredient, we recommend mixing and matching other toppings as you like!

We wrap rice and beans in a bun, just like classic burritos. But if you want very low-carb burrito bowls, you can skip the beans and use cauliflower rice as the base for the bowls.

Below are the **healthy and tasty ingredients** we used to make our Chipotle Chicken Burrito Bowl recipe.

For The Chipotle Chicken You Will Need:

- **Boneless chicken breasts** - or thighs if you prefer
- **Apple Cider Vinegar** - provides tang and acidity to tenderize meat quickly
- **Seasoning** - Chipotle pepper powder, ground cumin, dried oregano, garlic powder, salt, and pepper

The Ingredients You Need

1. Long Grain Rice - cooked according to package directions (or try broccoli or cauliflower rice)
2. Canned black beans - drained and heated

3. Canned Corn - Drained or cooked frozen corn that has been refrigerated

4. Guacamole - cooked or homemade guacamole

5. Salsa - whatever style and spiciness you want

6. Pico de Gallo - homemade or store-bought

7. Grated cheese - Mexican blend or cheddar

8. Sour cream – or Greek yogurt for a slightly healthier alternative

9. Shredded salad - Iceberg or romaine lettuce tastes best

10. Additional garnish - chopped cilantro, chopped chives, and lime wedges

How to make grilled chipotle chicken

This tried-and-true Chipotle Grilled Chicken recipe is quick and easy to make and can be prepared on an outdoor grill or stovetop.

- First, prepare a baking dish and a small bowl. Mix all the spices in the bowl with 1 tsp salt and ½ tsp ground black pepper (tsp = Teaspoon).

- Then place the chicken in the baking dish and pour the vinegar over the chicken. This adds flavor and helps the rub stick to the chicken, so don't skip it!

- Sprinkle the spice mixture over the chicken and rub on all sides to evenly coat.
- Heat the grill (or skillet) over medium heat, about 350 ° F. Grill the chicken for 5 minutes on each side until the internal temperature of the breast reaches 160° F.

Transfer the grilled chicken to a clean plate and let rest for 5 minutes. Then cut it into bite-sized pieces.

Assembling the Low-Carb Chipotle Chicken Burrito Bowls

Pro tip: For the tastiest and freshest chicken burrito bowls, add the hot ingredients to the bowls first.

Prepare 6 large bowls of soup or cereal. When you want to prepare a meal, take out 6 containers with lids. Pour about ¾ cup of cooked rice into each bowl. Then add ½ cup black beans and ¼ cup corn and up to 1 cup chipotle chicken over the rice. When you're ready to enjoy, top the Chipotle Chicken Burrito Bowls with guacamole, salsa, Pico de Gallo, shredded cheese, sour cream, leaves, cilantro, and a wedge of lime.

Summary And Instruction

Chipotle Chicken Burrito Bowls		
Prep Time	Cook Time	Total Time
20 Minutes	20 Minutes	40 Minutes

Ingredients

For the grilled chicken

1. 1 ½ pound boneless chicken breast or thighs
2. 1 teaspoon apple cider vinegar
3. 1 tbsp chipotle chili powder
4. 1 teaspoon ground cumin
5. 1 teaspoon dried oregano
6. ½ teaspoon garlic powder
7. Salt and pepper

For the burrito bowls - (all ingredients are optional)

1. 1 ½ cups long-grain rice
2. 2–15-ounce cans of black beans, drained and reheated
3. 15-ounce can of drained corn

4. ¾ cup guacamole

5. ¾ cup salsa of any type

6. ¾ cup Pico de Gallo

7. ¾ cup shredded mixed Mexican cheese

8. ½ cup sour cream

9. ½ cup shredded lettuce

10. ½ cup chopped cilantro and 1 lime cut into pieces

Instructions

For the rice:

1. Prepare a 4–6-liter saucepan. Put the rice in the pot. Then prepare according to the instructions on the package. (This usually means adding 3 cups of water and cooking for 15-20 minutes until you see air pockets on top of the rice.)

For the chicken:

1. Prepare a casserole dish and a small bowl. Mix all the spices in the bowl with 1 tsp salt and ½ tsp ground pepper.

2. Put the chicken in the casserole. Pour vinegar over the chicken. (This adds flavor and helps the rub stick to the chicken.) Sprinkle the cut mixture over the chicken and rub on all sides.

3. Heat a grill (or grill pan) over medium-high heat, about 350 degrees F. Grill the chicken for 5 minutes on each side. Let the chicken rest for 5 minutes, then cut it into bite-size pieces.

How to assemble the burrito bowls

1. Prepare 6 soup/cereal bowls. Place about ¾ cup of cooked rice in bowls. Add ½ cup black beans and ¼ cup corn. Place the chopped chipotle chicken over the rice. Top with guacamole, salsa, Pico de Gallo, grated cheese, sour cream, lettuce, cilantro, and a lime wedge.

NOTE

If you are prepping, I recommend leaving the cold toppings out of the bowls and storing them separately until ready to serve.

Premade Chipotle Grilled Chicken Burrito Bowls keep well in an airtight container in the fridge for 3-4 days.

You can freeze rotisserie chicken for even longer storage. Place the chilled ground chipotle chicken in a sealed, freezer-safe container and store it in the freezer for up to 3 months. Allow the chicken to thaw in the fridge overnight before assembling your bowls.

Nutrition Facts

Serving Size	1 bowl
Calories	518kcal
Carbohydrates	58g
Protein	34g
Fat	17g
Saturated Fat	66g
Trans Fats	1g
Cholesterol	96mg
Sodium	795mg
Potassium	880mg
Fiber	4g
Sugar	5g
Vitamin A	716IU
Vitamin C	12mg
Calcium	161mg
Iron	2mg

Meal Prep Plan #2:

Healthy Breakfast Hash

This healthy breakfast combines avocado and eggs for a balanced meal. It hits the mark every time, whether it's breakfast, lunch, or

dinner! Not only is this breakfast easy and delicious, but it also keeps me full and satisfied until lunch. That's why I have nothing to eat an hour later.

Best of all, this breakfast hash can be made in multiple servings, so you can easily spend the rest of the week on your own or have enough for the whole family. You can change things depending on what you have or what you like or don't like.

I often add extra veggies if I have some on hand. This recipe is a great way to clear out the fridge when you're nearing the end of the week and still have some cooking to do. The vegetables are a staple here every week for me, so something like this could easily come together.

Why The Breakfast Hash Is The Best For Meal Prep:

- It's perfect for any meal - breakfast, lunch, or dinner!
- It warms well!

- There are many ways to swap it out or combine it for different meals
- It is a satisfying and healthy meal

Ingredients You Need

- 4 cups of sweet potatoes (cut up into cubes)
- 2 cups Brussels (cup in half)
- 2 cloves garlic (finely chopped)
- 1/2 cup mushrooms
- 1/2 cup red onion
- 1 tablespoon olive oil, avocado oil, or avocado oil spray
- 1 teaspoon garlic powder
- 1 teaspoon sea salt and pepper
- Garnish with red pepper flakes and fresh cilantro or dill!
- Optional: Add 2-3 chicken and apple chicken sausages

How To Make It

1. Finely chop all the vegetables before you start. To speed up the cooking of sweet potatoes, microwave the whole potato for 2 minutes before doubling and sautéing.
2. Add 1 tablespoon of olive oil and 2 finely chopped garlic cloves in a bowl.

3. Add the sweet potatoes and sprouts to the pan and heat over medium heat.

4. Keep stirring while frying.

5. Add the remaining vegetables and further food over medium-low heat. Add the herbs.

6. Garnish with red pepper flakes and combine with eggs, avocado, or whatever you like.

Pro Tip#: I like to microwave my sweet potato for two minutes before slicing it so it's softer and easier to fry.

Variations For A Healthy Breakfast Hash

Mix things up by substituting vegetables and protein in this hash.

Protein: breakfast sausage, turkey sausage, or smoked bacon.

Vegetables: Peppers, regular potatoes, carrots, zucchini, slices of Swiss chard or Bok choy, asparagus, tomatoes.

What To Serve With Breakfast:

- Eggs. Try scrambled eggs, hard-boiled eggs, or egg jam with this hash.
- With breakfast sausages.
- Yogurt and fruit on the side.

Summary

Yield	4 Servings
Prep Time	10 Minutes
Cook Time	10 Minutes
Total Time	20 Minutes

This healthy breakfast hash is the perfect weeknight meal for an easy breakfast!

Approximate macros for 1 serving:

Calories	Protein	Fat	Carbs	Sodium	Sugar	Fiber
802g	42g	52g	43g	-	14g	19g

Meal Prep Plan #3:

20-Minute Meal-Prep Chicken, Rice, and Broccoli

Making this meal is a little bit tricky and you need to bring out your multitasking skills. While the chicken and rice cook, go ahead and

steam the broccoli. This can be done on the stove in a pot of boiling water or the microwave. All that remains is to carve the chicken, spoon the rice in and assemble the meal bowls.

Ingredients

For the rice:

- 2 cups of water
- 1 cup jasmine rice
- 3/4 tsp salt

For the chicken:

1. 4 small to medium boneless chicken breasts or thighs, about 4 oz each
2. 1 teaspoon brown or granulated sugar
3. 1/2 teaspoon paprika

4. 1/2 teaspoon cumin

5. 1/2 teaspoon garlic powder

6. Salt and pepper to taste

7. 1 tablespoon olive oil

8. 2-3cups broccoli sprouts

9. water for steaming

Instructions

1. To cook the Rice: Bring water to a boil in a medium saucepan. Stir in the rice; cover and reduce heat. Simmer for 15 minutes until all the water is absorbed.

2. To Cook the Chicken: Rub chicken with brown sugar, paprika, cumin, garlic powder, salt, and pepper. Heat 1-2 tablespoons of oil in a large, heavy-bottomed saucepan or skillet over medium heat.

3. Place the chicken in the skillet and fry on the first side for 5-6 minutes without stirring, until dark grill marks are visible on the underside. Flip the chicken breasts with tongs or a fork and cook the other side for 5-6 minutes. Turn off the heat and let the chicken breasts sit in the pan for at least 5 minutes before slicing.

4. Steamed Broccoli: There are two ways to cook broccoli. Blanch the broccoli on the stove. Boil water in a large saucepan. Add the broccoli florets to the skillet and blanch them for 1 minute only.

Remove from mold. To steam in the microwave: place the broccoli in a microwave-safe bowl and add 3 tablespoons of water to the bowl. Cover with a ceramic plate or plastic wrap. Microwave on high power for 3 minutes.

5. **Assembly:** Cut the chicken into slices or small pieces. Use a 1-cup measuring cup to evenly scoop 1 cup of rice into each (4 total). Top rice with chicken slices and broccoli florets. Cover and refrigerate for up to 4 days. Heat the microwave on the highest setting for 2 minutes or until steaming.

Nutritional Facts

Serving Size	1 serving
Calories	356kcal
Carbohydrates	41g
Protein	26g
Fat	9g
Saturated Fat Acids	2g
Cholesterol	107mg
Sodium	561mg

Potassium	474mg
Fiber	2g
Sugar	2g
Vitamin A	434 IU
Vitamin C	41mg
Calcium	48mg
Iron	2mg

Meal Prep Plan #4:

Bodybuilding Chicken Parmesan

This Bodybuilding Chicken Parmesan Recipe is quick, healthy, great for dinner, delicious, and LOADED with protein! The best  part? You only need a few ingredients to make it! The first thing you want to do is scoop out 1 1/2 pounds of chicken breasts, trim the fat, and cut them in half horizontally. The goal is to turn your chicken breasts into (thin!) chicken chops. This means you have two for each chicken breast. Reserve the chicken and take out 2 bowls. You want a small one for your wet mix and a bigger one for your dry mix.

Note that if you want to double or triple the recipe, you may need to use larger bowls. You can scale this Chicken Bodybuilding Recipe below!

- Add two extra-large egg whites and one tablespoon of olive oil to the small bowl. mix them up
- In the larger bowl, add 2/3 cup whole grapes and 8 tablespoons pink Parmesan. mix them up

- Once your wet and dry ingredients are ready to use, take out a baking dish or skillet. Coat it with nonstick cooking spray or line it with parchment paper for easy cleanup.

Before The Oven

- Place your thinly sliced chicken on your lined or lined casserole or skillet.
- Brush each piece with your wet (egg) mixture with a pastry brush. Be sure to coat both sides of your chicken.
- Don't have pastries? Do not worry! Place the chicken directly into the mixture.
- Once each piece is coated in your wet mixture, toss it several times in your dry mixture until completely coated. If you have any leftover dry mix, spread it over your chicken at the end.
- Now for the oven, spray the top of your chicken with nonstick cooking spray. This will give your Body Building Chicken Parmesan a nice crispy finish!
- Put the chicken in the oven at 232°C for 20 minutes.

Bodybuilding Chicken Parmesan Topping

- After 20 minutes, take them out and turn the pieces over.

- Spread 1/2 cup total pasta sauce and 3/4 cup total low-fat mozzarella cheese on top. Use the back of a spoon to spread your pasta sauce.
- If you want to spice things up a bit, add hot sauce or sriracha to your pasta sauce!
- Return to 45°F/232°C oven for 5-10 minutes or until cheese is melted.

Chicken Parmesan Tips

- ✓ To keep them crispy and not mushy, heat them in the oven (or toaster oven) at 350°F (176°C) for 10 to 15 minutes.
- ✓ Eat your Bodybuilding Parmesan in a sandwich, over pasta, rice, protein-rich quinoa, or just veggies if you're watching your carbs!

Ingredients

2. 1½ pounds chicken breasts
3. 2 extra large Egg whites
4. 1 tablespoon olive oil
5. ⅔ cup bread - whole grain
6. 8 tbsp parmesan cheese- Grated
7. ½ cup pasta sauce
8. ¾ cup mozzarella cheese - low fat

Instructions

1. Take out your chicken breasts, trim the fat and cut them in half (make them thin)
2. In a small bowl, combine egg white and olive oil
3. Mix them together
4. Place bread and parmesan in another large bowl
5. Mix them together
6. Take a baking sheet, grease it with a non-stick coating and place your chicken breasts on the baking sheet
7. Lightly brush your wet mixture on both sides of your chicken breast slices
8. Dip them in your dry mix
9. Coat the tops of your chicken breasts with nonstick cooking spray
10. Put them in the oven at 450°F (232°C) for 20 minutes
11. Take them out, turn them over, and evenly spread your pasta sauce and mozzarella cheese on top
12. Return to oven at 450°F (232°C) for another 5-10 minutes or until your cheese is melted.

Calories In The ENTIRE Recipe

Calories	1515kcal
Carbohydrates	55g
Fat	43g
Saturated Fat Acids	14g
Sodium	2010mg
Egg white	227 g
Glass	6g
Sugar	10g
Carbs	9.1g

Calories Per Serving (If You Make 6)

Calories	252kcal
Carbohydrates	9.1g
Fat	7.1gg
Saturated Fatty Acids	2.3g

Sodium	335mg
Protein	37.8g
Fiber	1g
Sugar	1.6g

Meal Prep Plan #5:

Easy Meal Prep Recipe Shrimp Fajita Bowls

The best meal recipes are the ones that get you in and out of the kitchen quickly with healthy meals for the week. That's why I love

this Shrimp Fajita Bowl. I use one of my favorite recipes, Sheet Pan Shrimp Fajitas to make these bowls. Quick preparation and easy cleaning.

Easy Meal Prep

Prepare the shrimp and peppers by cooking them quickly on a baking sheet. Reduce the preparation by buying shrimp already peeled and deveined. Cut the onion and peppers into thin slices so that they cook at the same speed as the shrimp. To make cleanup even easier, line the baking sheet with foil before baking.

Glass Meal Prep Containers

These containers are my favorites for the kitchen. They are divided into three sections to keep your food clean. They are also microwave and dishwasher-safe. These beautiful glass containers for food preparation can be found on Amazon.

Shrimp Fajita Bowl Meal Prep

Prep Time	Cook Time	Total Time	Course	Servings
10 mins	10 mins	20 mins	Main Course	4

Ingredients

- 1 1/2 pounds shrimp, peeled and deveined
- 1 yellow bell pepper, thinly sliced
- 1 red bell pepper, thinly sliced
- 1 orange bell pepper, thinly sliced
- 1 small red onion, thinly sliced
- 1 1/2 tablespoons extra virgin olive oil
- 1 teaspoon kosher salt
- several rings of freshly ground pepper
- 2 teaspoons chili powder
- 1/2 teaspoon garlic powder
- 1/2 teaspoon onion powder

- 1/2 teaspoon ground cumin
- 1/2 teaspoon smoked paprika powder
- Lime
- fresh cilantro for garnish
- 2 cups black beans
- 4 cups cooked cilantro-lime rice

Instructions

1. Preheat the oven to 450 degrees.
2. In a large bowl, combine the onion, paprika, shrimp, olive oil, salt and pepper, and spices.
3. Mix to combine.
4. Spray the baking sheet with nonstick cooking spray.
5. Spread the shrimp, peppers, and onions on a baking sheet.
6. Bake at 450 degrees for about 8 minutes. Then turn the oven to broil and cook for another 2 minutes or until the shrimp are cooked.
7. Squeeze the juice of fresh limes over the fajita mixture and garnish with fresh cilantro.
8. Cool the mixture of shrimp and peppers and divide into 4 ramekins.

Notes

If desired, remove the shrimp tails before cooking to facilitate serving.

Meal Prep Plan #6:

Workout Lasagna Individual Meal Prep

What if we told you that it is not necessary to give up Italian cuisine to have a summer figure? It's true! This lasagna recipe

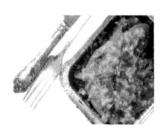 supports a workout routine for muscle growth and overall strength. Perfect for the bathing season!

Lasagna ingredients provide a high calorie, protein, and carbohydrate content, which is good for muscle building. This particular lasagna recipe is great because it's a cleaner version of your catering service lasagna and is made in multiple batches so it will last for multiple meals.

This workout lasagna is made with really basic ingredients like mushrooms, onions, turkey sausage, and lots of spices. It contains low-fat cottage cheese, mozzarella, and ricotta. One unusual ingredient that you might not expect is sweet potato, which adds nutritional value. Simply prepare and cook lasagna in multiple layers! This meal can last quite a long time and is a good addition to your diet.

Workout Lasagna Individual Meal Prep

Eat healthily and stay fit with this fantastic lasagna, individually prepared and ready to eat.

Yield	Serving Size	Course
6 people	1 Lasagna	Dinner and Lunch

Ingredients

- 1 pound ground turkey sausage
- 1/4 cup mushrooms, diced
- 1/4 cup red onion, diced
- 3 cloves of garlic, finely chopped
- 1 tablespoon fresh basil, chopped
- 1 tablespoon fresh oregano, minced
- 2 large tomatoes, cut into medium-sized cubes
- 15 ounces tomato sauce, no added sugar (unseasoned)
- 2 egg whites
- 1/2 cup low-fat cottage cheese
- 1/4 cup of low-fat ricotta cheese
- 3 tablespoons fresh parsley, finely chopped
- 1 teaspoon kosher salt

- 2 large sweet potatoes, thinly sliced
- 1 cup lean mozzarella, grated

Instructions

1. Preheat the oven to 400 degrees. Lightly spray pans with nonstick cooking spray and set aside.

2. Cook turkey sausage in a large skillet over medium-high heat. While cooking, break the sausage into small pieces. When there is no pinker in the sausage, add the mushrooms, onion, and garlic. Cook, stirring occasionally until the mushrooms and onions are tender. Combine basil, oregano, tomato, and tomato sauce in a mixing bowl. Bring the mixture to a boil, stirring constantly. Cook for 5 minutes, then remove from heat.

3. In a mixing bowl, whisk together egg whites, cottage cheese, ricotta, parsley, and salt. Mix well and set aside.

4. Place about 2 tablespoons of sausage sauce on the bottom of each serving plate. Place a layer of sweet potatoes on top, slightly overlapping each slice - about 4 slices per layer. Top with about 1/4 cup of sauce, followed by another layer of potatoes. Top with 1/4 cup cheese mixture and another layer of sweet potatoes. Repeat the layers (sauce, potatoes, cheese, and potatoes) until the pan is about 1/4

inch from the top of the pan. Sprinkle about 1/4 cup of shredded mozzarella on top.

5. Bake for 30 to 45 minutes until the potatoes are tender and the mozzarella is melted and lightly browned Once cooled, cover tightly and store in the fridge or freezer.

6. To reheat, lightly spray foil and cover lasagna with foil, sprayed side down. Bake for 20 to 30 minutes, until the lasagna is heated through.

Nutritional Facts

Serving	1 Lasagna
Calories	342 kcal
Fat	13g
Protein	27g
Saturated Fatty Acids	5g
Sodium	1113mg
Fiber	6g
Smart Points (freestyle)	5
Sugar	9g

| Carbs | 31g |
| Cholesterol | 79mg |

Meal Prep Plan #7:

Healthy Beef and Broccoli

Healthy beef and broccoli are classic dishes found in many Chinese restaurants. This quick and easy take on the classic stir-fry is a game-changer that will satisfy all your late-night cravings without the added refined sugar and sodium-laden MSG.

Beef broccoli is a little sweet, a little sticky, a little sour, and a whole lot delicious. It's layer upon layer of bold flavors, beautiful textures, and out-of-this-world flavors that come together in minutes to make the tastiest leftovers the next day.

Why The Steak And Broccoli Recipe Is Healthy For You

- **High Protein:** This is a protein-rich and healthy dinner with lean steak and broccoli!
- **Simple:** A short list of ingredients and minimal effort make this a satisfying comfort meal.
- **Low Carb:** Whether you're in your 30s, Paleo, or just leaner, this meal fits many healthy lifestyles.

- **A healthier variety:** No intense frying, no refined sugar, and less sodium than high-calorie broccoli at a meat restaurant!
- **Nutritious:** Broccoli is rich in fiber and vitamin C; lean meat is rich in vitamin B12 and rich in antioxidants. This stir-fried meal is ideal for dinner.

Ingredients For Healthy Beef And Broccoli

Beef: Rib, tri-section or roast beef, thinly sliced will work. Save the flank steak for the carne asada.

Tip for slicing the beef patty: Put the steak in the freezer for 15-20 minutes and then slice it while it's still very cold.

- **Broccoli & onion:** Cut the broccoli into florets and the onion into thin slices.
- **Cornstarch:** This is used to coat the meat. Combined with the frosting, it helps thicken.
- **For the frosting:** soy sauce (I use Bragg's Liquid amino). maple syrup or honey. If you like a little refined sugar, definitely use brown sugar. Finely chop the garlic and ginger.
- **Low sodium beef stock:** Use this to deglaze the pot so all the tasty bits get to the bottom.

- **Oil:** Avocado oil is excellent for frying. Both coconut oil and olive oil can be used, but keep in mind that the flavor profile may not be what you're looking for. Whatever you use must have a high smoke point.

What is the best frying oil? When cooking at high heat, the best oil is one with a high smoke point. The healthiest is avocado oil, which has a smoke point of 520 degrees F.

- Optional side dish: Chopped onion. Sesame seeds.

How to Make Healthy Beef and Broccoli

Prep: As with any stir-fry, you want to make sure all of your ingredients are chopped, minced, sliced, and ready to go. You move pretty fast, so it makes things a lot easier when you're done!

If you serve steak and broccoli with a side dish, e.g. Rice, you want to serve them at the same time.

- Make the sauce: Put the soy sauce, maple syrup, garlic, and ginger in a small bowl. Wipe it off and set it aside until it's time to add it.
- Coat Beef: Put the meat slices in a bowl and sprinkle cornstarch on top. Mix with tongs and brush well. Without the magic of starch, this sauce wouldn't be what we all know and love.

Why are corn stalks covered with beef in a pan? The cornmeal softens the meat and protects it from the hot pan.

- **Brown meat:** Heat a large ceramic frying pan and add oil. Swirl to coat. Add half of the meat and fry until nicely browned on all sides. Transfer to a plate, add a little oil to the pan, and repeat this step with the remaining beef. Cooking in batches allows for more even cooking and ensures that all sides get a nice brown finish.
- **Deglaze:** Return the pan to high heat and add the stock. Remove from the pan with a wooden spoon for a few minutes and scrape up any remaining bits that have stuck to the bottom of the pan. This gives the mixture a wonderful taste. Add the broccoli and onion and continue to cook for a few minutes.
- **Combine:** Remember that sauce you mixed earlier? What about the beef you put away? Take them both and put them away. Now let's cook! can you smell it? Reduce heat and simmer for up to 5 minutes. Stir frequently until the sauce has thickened. You don't want to overcook the broccoli. Crispy, crunchy broccoli is the texture we want!
- **Garnish and serve:** If you made your chosen pot of brown rice, quinoa, or pasta, it may already be ready.

More fun at home Steak and broccoli to-go: Serve it in cute little take-out boxes like you see on TV and let people use chopsticks forever!

Optional Add-ins and Variations

Broth Substitutes: Alternatives to different types of broth include chicken broth or vegetable broth, bone broth, or even water. Each gives a slightly different taste, but each gives you a delicious serving.

Broccoli stalks: Adding chunks of the stalk gives you a crunchier texture. It's very nutritious, especially when it's organic, and it's a great way to reduce waste. Peel, chop, and add. I always do this with salads or a healthy broccoli salad recipe. Do you like crunchy broccoli? Fry the broccoli first before adding it.

- **Other vegetables**: Snow peas, snow peas, peppers, carrots, or mushrooms can be used together, or - cooking times may vary.
- **Crush:** Use cashews or peanuts as a garnish, or toss drained and chopped water chestnuts into the pan after cooking is complete.
- **Heating:** red pepper flakes, black pepper, or a touch of cayenne pepper. instead
- **Orange juice:** Add to the sauce mixture for a little orange flavor.
- **Onion substitute:** You can use red onions if you have them on hand. If you buy this recipe at Target, be sure to opt for garlic. If you don't have any of the above, it's fine if you leave it entirely.

Sweetener: Personally, the honey flavor is a bit too strong in this dish, but give it a try and see what you think. Otherwise, try maple syrup or something else you use regularly, including sugar-free liquid sugar.

Dried ginger: If you don't have fresh ginger, use 1 teaspoon of dried ginger. This is another ingredient that you can omit if you don't have any and don't want to go to the store anymore.

Corn Starch Substitute: Arrowroot starch is a grain-free substitute.

Vegetable substitutes: Use tofu or mushrooms to keep this casserole vegan or vegetarian.

Tips for Best Results

Prepare: 'Stir fry' literally means cooking sliced, chopped, and sliced ingredients quickly over high heat, stirring constantly. Because of this constant stirring, you can't spend time slicing, chopping, or slicing along the way. Make sure everything is ready before lighting the stove and this will allow you to complete the process much faster.

Sodium content: If not using low-sodium broth, use 3 tablespoons of soy sauce.

Cooking utensils: If possible, use a non-stick ceramic pan. Wok cooking steams the food and a cast iron skillet uses a lot of oil. Even batch cooking helps achieve a nice brown finish.

The best oil: For sautéing, you should use an oil that is stable over high heat. While there are a few different oils that do this, we always look for oils that are also the healthiest and don't have overpowering flavors. The Avocado wins out!

How To Serve Beef With Broccoli

Traditional: Serve steak and broccoli with brown rice (or white rice) of your choice.

Other cereals: quinoa, buckwheat, millet, etc.

Lo Mein: includes ramen, egg noodles, spaghetti noodles, and rice noodles.

Low-carb: Serve with spaghetti squash or cauliflower rice. Cauliflower fried rice would be delicious!

How To Store Beef And Broccoli Stir Fry Recipe

Storage: Like takeout, this steak and broccoli dish won't last more than a day in the fridge. Store them in an airtight container and enjoy the extras the next day for a healthy lunch idea, but that's about it. Otherwise, the broccoli will become sticky.

Summary and Instruction

Healthy Beef And Broccoli

Easy to make, Healthy Beef and Broccoli Mash is a vegetarian dish filled with tender slices of beef, which are then coated in a sticky sauce that's low in sodium and sugar. Your favorite Asian snack is now healthier at home!

Servings	Calories	Prep Time	Cook Time	Total Time
4 Servings	325	15 Minutes	20 Minutes	35 Minutes

Equipment

1. Ceramic saucepan
2. Gauges
3. Measuring cup

Ingredients

- 1-pound flank, tri-tip, or sirloin steak that has been thinly sliced against the grain
- 1 kg broccoli, cut into florets
- 1/2 large white, thinly sliced
- 2 tablespoons oil for frying, use avocado oil
- 1 cup beef low-sodium beef broth
- 3 tablespoons soy sauce, use Bragg's Liquid Amino Acids
- 2 tablespoons of brown sugar, honey, or maple syrup
- 3 tablespoons cornstarch
- 1 tablespoon minced garlic
- 1 tablespoon chopped ginger
- 1 sprig of spring onion, chopped and optional for garnish
- 2 teaspoons sesame seeds, for garnish optional

Instructions

- Prepare all the ingredients for the beef and broccoli and start with the sides, such as rice, on the stovetop.
- Combine soy sauce, maple syrup, garlic, and ginger in a small bowl; Whisk with a fork and set aside.
- Place beef in a bowl, sprinkle with cornstarch, and toss well to coat with tongs.
- Preheat a large non-stick ceramic skillet over medium heat and add 1 tablespoon of oil to cover. Add half the beef and cook for about 3 minutes on each side or until nicely browned. Pour into a plate and set aside. Add the remaining 1 tablespoon of oil and repeat this step with the remaining half of the meat.
- Return the pan to high heat and add the broth. Drain in the pan for about 2 minutes. Add broccoli and onion, stir and cook for about 3 minutes.
- Add the sauce and the previously cooked beef. Reduce the heat to medium and cook for 3 to 5 minutes, stirring often, until the sauce has thickened. Beef cornstarch is added to the sauce and thickens it. But don't overcook the broccoli.
- Garnish with spring onions and sesame seeds. Serve hot over brown rice, quinoa, or pasta of your choice.

NOTES

- **Storage:** Up to 24 hours in the refrigerator in an airtight container (the broccoli becomes too sticky afterward). Boil some beef stock or water on the stove until hot.

- **Freezing:** I don't recommend freezing it.

- **Broth:** Reduce soy sauce to 2 tbsp if using low-sodium beef broth. You can use any other broth or broth, for example, B. chicken, vegetables, or even water.

- **Garlic Substitute:** This is a great addition to the skillet, but you can leave it out or use red onion.

- **Sweetener:** I found the honey a little too strong for my taste. But you can use it. If you regularly use a sugar-free sweetener, such as B. erythritol, feel free to use it.

- **Dried ginger:** Use 1 tsp instead of fresh or leave it completely.

Corn Starch Substitute: Arrowroot starch is a grain-free substitute.

Soy Substitute: Use Coconut Amino Acids

Nutritional Facts

15-Minute Walk To Healthy Beef And Broccoli		
Serving	1.5 cups	% Daily Value
Calories	350 kcal	
Fat	12g	18%
Saturate Fat	3g	15%
Monounsaturated Fat	6g	"
Polyunsaturated Fat	27g	"
Carbohydrate	20g	7%
Sodium	854mg	36%
Fiber	12g	12%
Protein	41g	82%
Sugar	7g	8%
Potassium	972mg	28%
Cholesterol	104mg	35%

Iron	4mg	22%
Vitamin A	706IU	14%
Vitamin C	85mg	103%
Calcium	112mg	11%

Meal Prep Plan #8:

Meal Prep High-Protein Italian Pasta Bake

This dish is ridiculously quick to prepare (literally throw all the ingredients in the oven and bake for 10 minutes) and it only takes

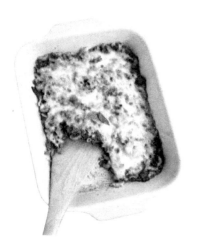

a few ingredients - but you'll never know. It's delicious, nutritious, and even tastier the next day - truly the best of both worlds!

And the best? Not only is this recipe ideal for weekend prep, but it can feed and delight a crowd! Serve it at the next fall meeting. No one will

believe how little time it took to open! Sneaky, sane hearts, anyone?

Although I love a well-prepared meal, sometimes the simplest recipes are the best. And if your days are anything like mine, this super satisfying, healthy, high-protein version of a classic is for you. Make your life easier this season and avoid spending time in the kitchen! Wouldn't you rather spend it enjoying all the fun fall activities?

Ingredients

- 4 ounces of Banza pasta
- 1 pound ground beef
- 1 dl frozen sliced paprika and onion
- 1 dl marinara sauce
- 2 tablespoons Italian (or pizza) seasoning
- 1 large egg
- 1 dl grated mozzarella

Instructions

1. Preheat oven to 350 degrees F. Cook noodles according to directions. Drain the water and set it aside.

2. Meanwhile, in a large skillet, brown the ground beef, stirring with a wooden spoon. When the meat is ready, add the bell pepper and onions, and pizza flavoring to the casserole.

3. Once the meat mixture is well blended, place it in a large mixing bowl along with the pasta, marinara sauce, and egg. Mix the ingredients well.

4. Place the ingredients in a small rectangular (or square) baking dish and sprinkle with mozzarella.

5. Bake for 10 minutes or until cheese is completely melted.

6. Serve immediately!

Nutritional Information

Serving Size	Fat	Carbohydrates	Protein
4	16	21	32

Meal Prep Plan #9:

White Bean Turkey Chili

A delicious and creamy white Bean Turkey Chili recipe made with canned beans, ground turkey, seasonings, and herbs - no tomatoes!

This easy chili can be made on the stovetop, slow cooker, or Instant Pot. Leftovers are even better for lunch the next day!

My friend Sophia shared this recipe, which I've adapted over the years, and I remember asking her if she forgot to tell me about the tomatoes. No, no tomatoes in this chili, which I remember driving me crazy. It's very common to see a white chili recipe these days, so I'm sure you won't be surprised. That's a lot, you can make a batch for dinner and freeze the leftovers for another night.

Toppings are optional, you can do it with whatever you want on your chili. Here are some suggestions:

Chili Toppings:

- Crushed chips

- Sour cream or Greek yogurt

- cilantro or spring onions

- Chopped green onion or red onion

- Sliced avocado

- Monterey Jack, Pepper Jack, or Cheddar cheese

Notes

I prefer the 93% lean ground turkey flavor, but you can get leaner with 99% which lowers the WW score. To make them dairy-free, you can omit the sour cream. If you prefer, replace the ground turkey with ground beef. Yogurt solidifies during cooking, if you prefer to use yogurt, use it as a filling.

Freezing and Reheating Chili:

Let the chili cool and place it in a freezer-safe container. Place in the fridge to warm in the evening before cooking, then again on the stove or in the microwave.

Ingredients

- olive oil spray
- 2 small onions, chopped
- 5 garlic cloves, minced
- 3 pounds 93% lean ground turkey
- 1 4.5 oz diced green chiles
- 1/2 teaspoon kosher salt
- 1/2 tablespoon cumin
- 1/2 tablespoon of oregano
- 2 teaspoons chili powder to taste
- 1/2 to 2 teaspoons crushed red pepper flakes to taste
- 1 bay leaf
- 4 cannellini or kidney beans from 15.5-ounce cans, rinsed and drained
- 2 cups chicken broth

- 1/2 cup low-fat sugar or Greek yogurt

Optional Toppings:

- Monterey Jack or Pepper Jack cheese, grated
- avocado dice
- Coriander
- sliced jalapenos
- Greek yogurt or sour cream
- sliced spring onion

Instructions

1. Heat a large heavy skillet or Dutch oven over medium heat. When hot, drizzle with oil.
2. Add onion and garlic, and sauté until soft, about 4-5 minutes.
3. Add meat and cook until white and cooked through, about 5 minutes.
4. Add diced green chiles, salt, cumin, oregano, chili powder, and red pepper flakes and cook for 2 minutes.
5. In a blender, puree 1 can of beans with 1 cup of broth. Add to pot with remaining beans, broth, and bay leaves and bring to a boil.

6. Cover and simmer, stirring occasionally, until thickened and flavors blend about 30 to 35 minutes.

7. Stir in sour cream and cook for 4-5 minutes. Adjust spices and salt to taste.

8. Garnish with your favorite toppings before serving.

9. Slow Cooker Preparation: To prepare in the slow cooker, follow steps 1-5, reduce broth to 1 1/2 cups, and place in the slow cooker on low heat for 8 hours.

10. Instant Pot Instructions: To brew in the Instant Pot, you will need an 8-quart IP or half the recipe. Reduce broth to 1 1/2 cups, and pressure cook for 25 minutes.

White Bean Turkey Chili	
Prep Time	10 Minutes
Cook Time	1 Hour
Total Time	1hr 10 minutes
Yield	12 servings
Cals	307
Protein	25
Carbs	12
Fats	30
Course	Dinner, Lunch
Cuisine	American

Meal Prep Plan #10:
Easy Vegan Meal Prep Bowls

Maybe you try to eat meat only in the evening, avoid meat for breakfast, or just attend Meatless Monday every week. Either way, these meal preps will definitely come in handy. With these bowls, you can change your eating routine every week.

Why You'll Love These Meal Prep Bowls

All four recipes are quick to prepare, so you won't have to spend hours cooking in the coming week. There are four different flavor options depending on your preference (or try them all!) Each bowl contains a healthy amount of protein to keep you full and satisfied all afternoon

How To Make Vegan Meals

Three out of four meals start with a base, either pasta, quinoa, or rice, and that's usually a good place to start.

Start by preparing the base

For the tofu dish: Fry the tofu, then roast the broccoli. Ideally, the rice, tofu, and broccoli will be ready around the same time, but don't worry if they aren't, especially if you're making these dumplings ahead of time. Simply add all ingredients to any of the meal preps, sprinkle over sriracha, and refrigerate

For the lentil Bolognese: While the pasta is cooking, prepare the lentil, Bolognese. First off, this recipe is pretty easy because it's a one-pot meal, so you put everything in a pot and simmer for 20 minutes or until the lentils are soft. Then you may pour everything into the containers you'll need for dinner prep.

Of all the meal bowls, quinoa bowls are probably the quickest to make. While the quinoa cooks, heat the beans in a pan on the stove and sauté the bell pepper with the seasoning in a pan. You can also cook the tomatoes, but I chose to leave them raw. Then add the quinoa, tomatoes, beans, and pepper to a bowl. I recommend waiting just before eating before cutting the avocado! But if you have half an avocado left, just put it in a small plastic bag and container and it should stay fresh for at least 24 hours.

For the sweet potato casserole, all you need to do is roast the sweet potatoes and heat the peas on the stove. Depending on your personal preference, you can leave the skin on the potato or peel it. But be sure to rinse the chickpeas to remove any moisture from the can.

Ingredients Substitution

Although these bowls are fine for use, feel free to replace and/or change them as you see fit. Some examples are:

- Turn on the base
- Use another vegetable for the sweet potato dish and/or roast the chickpeas
- Add the tempeh/seitan to the quinoa bowl
- Including vegan cheese in lentil Bolognese
- And more!

Honestly, there are plenty of options when it comes to vegan meal trays, so get as creative as you want! They're also a great way to use up ingredients that have been sitting in the fridge for a while.

Ingredients

For the tofu rice bowl

- See below

for the Bolognese lentils

See below

for the Mexican quinoa bowls

- 4 cups cooked quinoa
- 1 can (14 oz) black beans, drained and rinsed
- 1 sliced avocado
- 1 cup grape tomatoes, sliced
- 2 bell peppers, sliced and seeded
- ½ teaspoon garlic powder
- ½ teaspoon smoked paprika powder
- cilantro for garnish

for the sweet potato dumplings

- 4 roasted sweet potatoes
- 2 cans (14 oz each) of chickpeas, drained and washed
- 3 cups peas
- any sauce or dressing (I used mild buffalo sauce)

for the Mexican quinoa bowls:

1. Cook the quinoa on the stove as usual. Meanwhile, drain and rinse the black beans, put them in a small saucepan, and cook over medium heat for a few minutes.
2. Place the pepper strips in a bowl, drizzle with 1 teaspoon of olive oil, garlic powder, and smoked paprika, and stir. Place

the peppers in a skillet and sauté for a few minutes until soft. While the peppers cook, slice the tomatoes.

3. To serve: Divide cooked quinoa among 4 meal prep containers (see below) and top with black beans, tomatoes, cooked peppers, and avocado. Optional: Sprinkle with cilantro.

for the sweet potato bowls:

1. Preheat the oven to 400°. Cut the sweet potato into wedges and place it on a baking tray lined with baking paper. Roast sweet potatoes for 8 minutes, then flip and roast for another 8 minutes or until soft.

2. While the potatoes are frying, cook the peas. When the potatoes are ready, add them to the bowl with the cooked peas. Finally, pour the chickpeas into a colander, rinse well and add to the feeding bowl. Drizzle with your favorite dressing or condiment (I used buffalo sauce) and enjoy!

Notes

The meal is an estimate and should be calculated based on the dish you are preparing

Nutritional Information

Calories	613 calories
Carbs	111g
Fat	12g
Saturated fatty acids	2g
sodium	151mg
potassium	1803mg
Fiber	23g
sugar	21g
Vitamin A	35264 IU
Vitamin C	135mg
Calcium	140mg
Iron	mg

Meal Prep Plan #11:

Chicken Shawarma Quinoa Bowls

Ready in less than 30 minutes, these CHICKEN SHAWARMA Quinoa

Bowls are the perfect introduction to the great flavors and spices of Middle Eastern cuisine. Marinated in a blend of everyday herbs and spices, the result is a luscious, complex, and deliciously flavorful chicken dinner that's perfect for a week of meal prep!

The taste, color, and aroma of Middle Eastern cuisine make it a favorite and include recipes like Moroccan Beef Tagine with Eggplant, Persian Cranberry Rice Pilaf, and Easy Pan Sumac Chicken with roasted vegetables.

What Is Chicken Shawarma?

If you Google, Wikipedia tells you that chicken shawarma is a ..." meat preparation, where lamb, chicken, turkey, beef, veal, or mixed meats are placed on a spit... and you can grill it for up to a day."

This chicken is so delicious and smells so good that the whole neighborhood will come to your house asking for the recipe.

Chicken Shawarma Marinade Ingredients

Marinade and marinating time are IMPORTANT. Try the marinade overnight to absorb the flavor and spices.

- Lemon juice (the real one, not the fake one)
- Garlic
- Cumin
- Paprika
- salt + pepper
- Cayenne (not much, but a little)
- Cinnamon
- Cardamom
- Olive oil

I assume you already have at least half of these ingredients on hand. Yes? Nope? no idea? It's good. A spice drawer is also a scary place for me.

Best Ways To Cook Chicken Shawarma

There are several ways to cook chicken shawarma. As I believe most of us don't have a vertical spit, we'll have to settle for one of the below

- BBQ or grill
- Bake
- Pan Fry

When it comes to cooking meat, I think it's best to go with what you do best. Or whatever is easiest for you at the time. In other words, there is no "best" way to make chicken shawarma.

I like chicken myself. It's more reliable than frying in a pan and less multitasking. When I made these quinoa bowls with the intention of using the leftovers to make meals, I made it with my 5-year-old at home. It is not easy. And so the oven is my friend.

How To Serve Chicken Shawarma

I'll tell you a secret... there's no right way. Anyway, I've never encountered a wrong way. However, I do have some recommendations on what to eat chicken shawarma with or on or...

In a salad bowl. I leave this very wide and open to your own personal interpretation. Because today I made a bowl of quinoa with cucumber yogurt, but who says tomorrow I won't serve it with cabbage and rice?

Wrapped up. There really is nothing better in life than chicken shawarma wrapped in soft, fluffy Middle Eastern strips. When I lived in Germany, doner kebab was everywhere and became my go-to for a light dinner.

Like a chicken coop. Chicken, fresh vegetables, hot bread, hummus... In other words, do what makes you happy.

Why Chicken Shawarma Is An Easy Meal Prep Idea

- Chicken and marinade can easily be prepared in bulk
- It's quick and easy to do
- It can be served in several ways

- Ingredients stay fresh all week (translation - no soggy mess).

Shawarma Chicken Quinoa Bowls are a great way to cook on Sunday and pack lunch for the week.

In each bowl, I added -

- Mixed vegetables
- Tomatoes and cucumber
- Quinoa
- Chickpeas
- Lemon

Chicken Shawarma Quinoa Bowl	
Prep Time	10 Minutes
Cook Time	20 Minutes
Marinate	4 hrs.
Total Time	30 Minutes
Course	Lunch, Main Course, Meal Prep, Salad
Cuisine	Middle Eastern

Servings	6
Calories	722 Kcal

Ingredients

lb. of boneless thighs

For The Marinade

- 4 tablespoons of olive oil
- 2 lemons - squeezed
- 6 cloves garlic - minced
- 1 teaspoon of cumin
- 2 teaspoons of paprika
- 2 teaspoons of salt
- 1 teaspoon freshly ground black pepper
- ½ teaspoon cayenne pepper
- ¼ teaspoon ground cinnamon
- 1 teaspoon ground cardamom

For The Cucumber Tahini Yogurt

- 2 cups of Greek yogurt
- 4 tablespoons of tahini
- 1 clove garlic - minced

- 1 tablespoon lemon juice
- ½ cup cucumber - grated

To Serve

- 2 cups cooked quinoa
- 2 heads romaine lettuce - finely chopped
- ½ cup spring onions - chopped
- 4 Roma tomatoes - diced
- 1 can chickpeas - drained and rinsed
- 2 avocados - peeled and sliced
- 1 large English cucumber – sliced
- Fresh lemon, mint, and sesame - for garnish

Instructions

For Chicken And Marinade

1. Whisk all marinade ingredients together in a large bowl until well blended. Transfer the marinade to a large Ziplock bag.
2. Carefully transfer the chicken to the bag. Remove all of the air from the bag by sealing it tightly. Gently turn the marinated chicken over. making sure every part of each piece of chicken is coated in the marinade.

3. Place the chicken in the refrigerator to marinate for at least 2 hours, preferably overnight.

4. When ready to cook, remove the chicken from the refrigerator and preheat the oven to 375 degrees F. Line a baking sheet with parchment paper. Place the chicken on the baking sheet, using 2 sheets if necessary (do not overfill the baking sheet, as the chicken will cook less well).

5. Bake at 375 degrees F for about 20 minutes or until the internal temperature reads 165 degrees with a digital thermometer. Remove from the oven and let the chicken rest.

For The Cucumber-Tahini Yogurt

1. Place all the ingredients for the cucumber tahini yogurt in a medium bowl and mix well. Taste and refrigerate until ready to serve.

For The Quinoa Bowls

1. While the chicken is cooking, prepare the ingredients for the quinoa bowls. Divide the lettuce, quinoa, tomato, chickpeas, avocado, and cucumber into each bowl. Garnish with fresh mint, sesame, and lemon. Top each bowl with chicken kebab slices and cucumber tahini yogurt.

For The Meal Prep Bowls

1. If you are making them in meal bowls or if you have leftovers, the same idea for building a meal bowl as for making a salad bowl applies. Just decide which ingredients you want in each container and arrange them accordingly.

Nutritional Information

Calories: 722 calories | Carbohydrates: 48g | Protein: 56g | Fat: 36g | Saturated fatty acids: 5g | Cholesterol: 182mg | Sodium: 1212mg | Potassium: 1879mg | Fiber: 16g | Sugar: 8g | Vitamin A: 1995 IU | Vitamin C: 44.2mg | Calcium: 248mg | Iron: 7.3mg

(Nutritional information listed is approximate and will vary depending on the cooking method and specific brands of ingredients used.)

Printed in Great Britain
by Amazon

24110563R00053